# 101 ANIMAL SECRETS

All rights reserved. Published by Scholastic Inc., *Publishers since 1920.*
SCHOLASTIC and associated logos are trademarks and/or registered trademarks
of Scholastic Inc.

ISBN-13: 978-0-545-05122-4
ISBN-10: 0-545-05122-3

20 19 18 17 16 15 14 13 12 11                                    13

Printed in the U.S.A.    40
First printing, January 2009
Book design by Kay Petronio

# 101 ANIMAL SECRETS

BY Melvin + Gilda Berger

SCHOLASTIC

The albatross has the largest wingspan of any bird. Because of its huge wings, the albatross can glide for months on ocean winds without landing. This giant bird soars through the air at about 25 miles an hour (40.2 kph). It can even sleep while flying.

# #1 AN ALBATROSS CAN FLY FOR A YEAR WITHOUT STOPPING

# #2 ALLIGATORS POP THEIR EYES IN AND OUT

An alligator has two eyes that stick out on top of its head. The eyes let the alligator hunt for animals on land while swimming in the water. But if an enemy attacks, the alligator can pull its eyes down into its skull. As soon as the danger passes, the alligator pops its eyes out again.

Ants are small—but they are very strong for their size. If you were that strong, you could lift an automobile. The ants carry or drag heavy loads of food back to their nests. The food may be parts of plants or bits of dead animals.

#3 ANTS CAN LIFT 50 TIMES THEIR WEIGHT

# #4 AN ANTEATER'S TONGUE IS AS LONG AS YOUR ARM

The anteater flicks its very long tongue into an ant nest. Hundreds of ants get caught on its sticky surface. The anteater then pulls the tongue back into its long snout and slurps down all the ants. In less than a second, the animal is ready to catch more ants.

The Arctic fox lives near the icy North Pole. In winter, the fox's fur turns white, which helps the animal hide in the snow. It also makes it easier for the fox to escape its enemies and catch the animals it hunts. In spring, the fox's coat changes to brown—a color that matches the soil under the melted snow.

# #5 THE ARCTIC FOX CHANGES COLOR TWICE A YEAR

# #6 THE BASILISK LIZARD WALKS ON WATER

The basilisk lizard scampers across ponds or streams to flee danger. It races on its hind legs across the water. Some say that fringes on the lizard's hind toes trap bubbles of air under its feet. This keeps it from sinking if it runs fast enough. Basilisks have been said to run across water for distances of up to 100 feet (30.5 m).

Bats can find their way in the dark much better than you can. They make high squeaking sounds and listen for the echoes. An echo that bounces back quickly tells them that an object is nearby. Echoes that take longer mean that the object is farther away. This way of "seeing" lets bats find the insects they eat—without bumping into walls or trees.

# #7 BATS CAN "SEE" IN THE DARK

# #8 A BEAVER NEVER STOPS GROWING

Beavers keep getting longer and heavier until they die—usually at about 12 years of age. The beavers' bright orange front teeth also grow without stopping. Beavers use these very strong teeth to cut down trees and eat the bark. They also build dams and homes in the water with the branches.

A bee's stinger is located at the end of its body. The stinger has little hooks along the sides. When the bee stings a person or animal, a painful poison flows into the victim. As the bee flies away, though, the hooks hold on. The stinger pulls out of the bee's body. Without its stinger, the bee soon dies.

# #9 MOST BEES STING ONCE— THEN DIE

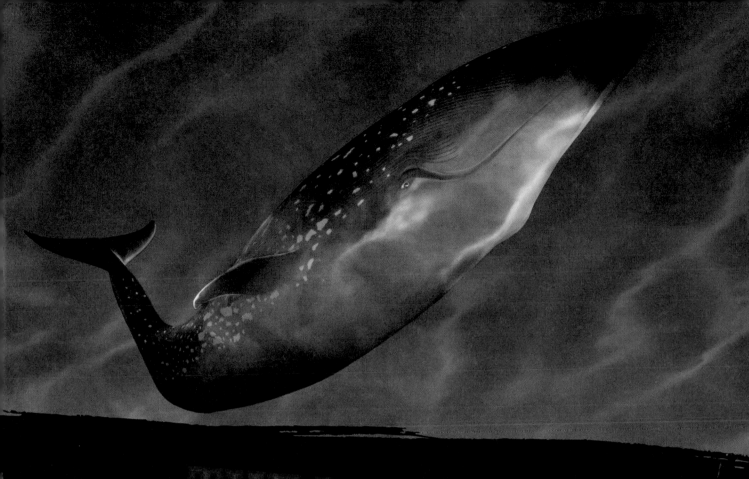

# 10 THE BLUE WHALE'S HEART IS THE SIZE OF A SMALL CAR

Everything about the blue whale is gigantic. Its body weighs as much as 25 elephants, is as long as three buses, and is as high as a 2-story building! Fifty people could stand on its tongue. Its stomach can hold more than a ton (1.1 t) of food. The blue whale is by far the biggest animal that ever lived.

True buffalo are found only in India and parts of Africa—not in North America. The large animals that we call buffalo are actually bison. Bison have humped shoulders and huge heads and necks. They are bigger than true buffalo. The bison's long hair also makes it look different from the buffalo.

# #11 THE AMERICAN BUFFALO IS REALLY A BISON

# #12 BULLS ARE COLOR-BLIND

Many people believe that bulls charge a bullfighter's cape because it is bright red. In fact, bulls cannot tell one color from another. To get the bull's attention, the bullfighter shakes his cape. The bull charges the cloth because it is waving, not because it is red.

A butterfly starts life as an egg that a female butterfly lays on a leaf. In time the egg hatches and a wormlike caterpillar crawls out. The caterpillar is the baby butterfly. It grows bigger and bigger. One day, it disappears into a shell that it builds around itself. After some months, a fully grown butterfly breaks out and flies away.

# #13 A BABY BUTTERFLY LOOKS LIKE A WORM

# #14 A CAMEL'S HUMPS HOLD NO WATER

The camel's humps are filled with fat, not water. The fat in the humps gives the camel energy when it does not have enough to eat. The camel gets the water it needs from eating its food and drinking. It loses hardly any water by sweating, so a camel can go days or weeks without anything to drink.

A cat can fall or jump from a treetop or high building and land safely. That's because it spreads its legs apart and flattens its body, much like a parachute. It also bends its legs to lessen the shock of striking the ground. One report tells of a cat dropped from an airplane flying at 800 feet (244 m). It landed on its feet and was able to walk away.

A CAT CAN FALL FROM A GREAT HEIGHT AND NOT GET HURT

#15

# #16 CENTIPEDES DON'T HAVE 100 LEGS

*Centipede* means "100 legs." But you'll never find a centipede with exactly that number. These worm-like animals have anywhere from 30 to more than 350 legs. The two legs behind its head are formed into fangs. They contain poison that the centipede uses to catch and kill worms and insects—and sometimes even bigger animals.

You may think that chameleons change color to blend into their surroundings. But chameleons actually change color because they are scared. Chameleons also change when they feel too hot or cold, want to attract a mate, or go from shade to sunlight. The change may take a few seconds or occur more slowly.

# #17 CHAMELEONS CHANGE COLOR WHEN SCARED

# #18 THE CHEETAH IS THE FASTEST LAND ANIMAL

The cheetah is built for speed, with a streamlined body and long, thin legs. When chasing prey, a cheetah can reach a speed of about 70 miles an hour (112 kph). That's more than the speed limit for cars on most superhighways. But a cheetah can keep that top speed for only a short distance.

Like most birds, chickens are able to fly. But chickens can't fly very far—only a few feet (1 m) at a time—or very high. They are too heavy. Chickens fly mainly to escape enemies, such as dogs or foxes. Flying is also how chickens get over fences or reach the perches on which they roost at night.

19 CHICKENS CAN FLY

# 20 CHIMPANZEES "SMILE" WHEN SCARED

When a chimpanzee shows its teeth, you may think it is smiling. But really the chimpanzee is probably scared or frightened. A happy chimpanzee only shows its bottom teeth. Watch out, though, for a chimpanzee that holds its two lips tightly together. It may be getting ready to attack.

Snake charmers play their pipes and pretend to charm cobra snakes with their music. The snakes "dance," even though they have no ears and cannot hear the music. They sway because they are following the movements of the snake charmers.

# #21 COBRAS ARE DEAF

# #22 CRICKETS HEAR WITH THEIR KNEES

A cricket's ears are not where you'd expect them to be. They are under the knees of the cricket's front legs. Each ear is a tiny hole with a tight, thin cover. Crickets pick up sounds through these little openings. Only male crickets make sounds. They do it by rubbing their wings together.

Crocodiles cry—but not because they are sad or hurt. Crocodiles shed tears to clean their eyes. This also kills any germs that are there. A little gland near their eyes does the job. When people say someone is "crying crocodile tears," they mean that he or she is just pretending to be sad.

# 23 CROCODILES CRY

# #24 CUCKOOS ARE LAZY

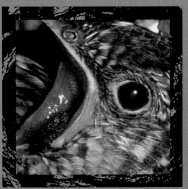

Cuckoo birds often lay their eggs in the nests of other birds. This way, the cuckoo avoids the hard work of building a nest. The other birds sit on the cuckoos' eggs until they hatch. Then the other birds even feed the baby cuckoo—just as they would feed their own babies.

The best-known chicken-sized dinosaur was compsognathus (komp-SOG-na-thus). It was only 2 feet (0.6 m) long—and most of that length was in its tail! Experts believe there were many more small dinosaurs than large ones. But they think that most small dinosaur fossils were destroyed and are lost forever.

# #25 MOST DINOSAURS WERE THE SIZE OF CHICKENS

# #26 DOGS DREAM

Have you ever noticed a dog bark, whine, or twitch while asleep? Scientists tell us that these are signs that the dog is dreaming. They also find that dogs sometimes have REM, or Rapid Eye Movement, while asleep. Since humans have REM while dreaming, it seems likely that dogs dream just as you do.

Dolphins are among the brightest of all animals. They can learn all sorts of tricks. Trainers can teach them to play catch with a ball or jump through hoops. On command, they can leap high in the air or find things in the water.

DOLPHINS ARE VERY SMART

27

# #28 DRAGONFLIES CAN FLY LIKE HELICOPTERS

A dragonfly is an insect that can do almost anything that a helicopter can do. This insect can hover, or stay in one place in the air. It can make sudden sharp turns, fly backward, and even roll over while flying. A dragonfly can also fly faster than any other insect. The fastest can reach a speed of about 35 miles an hour (56 kph).

A bald eagle, which is the symbol of the United States, is not really bald. Its head is covered with white feathers, while the feathers on the rest of its body are dark brown. No one is sure where the bald eagle got its name. Perhaps it's because you cannot see its white head feathers from far away—so the eagle looks bald.

# #29 EAGLES ARE NOT BALD

# THE ELEPHANT USES ITS TRUNK AS A HOSE

# #30

An elephant doesn't drink water through its trunk, as you may think. It uses its trunk to squirt water into its mouth, or as a hose to wash or cool off. Mainly, the trunk is the animal's nose for breathing and smelling. An elephant can also pick up almost anything with its trunk, from a peanut to a huge log.

Fireflies are not flies, and they are not bugs. Fireflies are beetles. Flies and bugs suck up liquids, but beetles eat solid foods. Fireflies get their name from the flashes of light they produce. The light comes from chemicals that they mix inside their bodies. Even though fireflies are not bugs, they are often called lightning bugs.

#31 FIREFLIES ARE NOT FLIES

# #32 FLIES LAY HUNDREDS OF EGGS AT A TIME

The world has trillions of flies. That's because one female fly can lay as many as 250 tiny eggs at a time! And she lays eggs about 4 times during her life. The eggs of the offspring result in a million or so new flies. On and on it goes, with millions of flies multiplying very fast.

A flounder is a flat fish that lives on the ocean bottom. When a flounder egg hatches, the baby is born with two ordinary eyes—one on each side of its head. But as the fish grows, one of the eyes slowly moves to the same side as the other eye. Soon both eyes are on the top side of the fish as it looks up from the bottom of the sea.

# #33 THE FLOUNDER HAS TWO EYES ON ONE SIDE OF ITS HEAD

# #34 A FROG SWALLOWS WITH ITS EYES

A frog shoots out its long, sticky tongue to catch the insects and small animals it feeds on. To swallow the food, the frog blinks its bulging eyes. This pushes the huge eyeballs down on the top of its mouth, which squeezes the food into its throat.

Everyone knows that giraffes are very tall. But here's a well-kept secret. The giraffe has a long, blue tongue that measures almost 2 feet (0.6 m) in length. That's long enough to reach around and touch the giraffe's ears. A giraffe's neck alone can be over 8 feet (2.4 m) long. Yet a giraffe has only seven neck bones—the exact same number that you do.

# #35 A GIRAFFE CLEANS ITS EARS WITH ITS TONGUE

# #36 A GOOSE CAN'T SEE STRAIGHT!

A goose has eyes on the sides of its head, which makes it hard to see straight ahead. That's partly why geese fly in giant V formations. They see the birds flying to their sides better than they see the birds in front or back of them. Flying in formation also helps saves energy for the geese behind the leader.

Many people think that gorillas are fierce, violent animals. Nothing could be further from the truth. In the wild, gorillas are really quiet, peaceful plant-eaters, with few enemies other than humans. Male gorillas may stand up and beat their chests or roar when angry. But they rarely attack people or other animals.

# #37 GORILLAS ARE SHY

# HARES LOOK LIKE RABBITS—BUT THEY'RE NOT RABBITS

## #38

You may have heard that hares and rabbits are the same animal. But they are not. Hares are bigger than rabbits and have much longer ears. When in danger, hares hop away at high speed. Rabbits hide or freeze in place. Then they hop away about half as fast as hares do.

If hens sat on their eggs, the shells might break. So hens just squat over the eggs to keep them warm. Hens lay about 250 eggs a year. Farmers find that hens lay more eggs when music is playing in the chicken coop or when the lights are on all the time.

HENS DON'T SIT ON THEIR EGGS

#39

# A HIPPOPOTAMUS'S YAWN MAY MEAN TROUBLE

# #40

Often, hippos look as though they are yawning. They open their mouths very wide and show their huge teeth. But the yawn may be something else. It may be a warning to another hippo, a lion, or a crocodile to stay away—or be ready to fight.

The horned toad is really a small lizard with a special way of defending itself. When under attack by a coyote, for example, the horned toad squirts real blood from its eyes. The blood startles and scares the coyote. The coyote lets go of the toad and runs away. The little horned toad—only about 5 inches (13 cm) long—can squirt blood for up to a yard (1 m).

# #41 THE HORNED TOAD SQUIRTS BLOOD FROM ITS EYES

# #42 HORSES SLEEP STANDING UP

A horse's legs lock in place when the animal falls asleep. That's why the horse does not topple over while it is sleeping. Experts say horses sleep on their feet for a good reason. In case of danger they can flee quickly, without taking time to stand up first.

Howler monkeys live in the dense jungles of Central and South America. They shriek to mark their territory or to signal danger. The howlers make the sound by forcing air through an extra-large, hollow bone in the throat. Their shrill screams can be heard from more than a mile (1.6 km) away. Male howlers are much louder than females.

# #43 HOWLER MONKEYS SHRIEK

# HUMMINGBIRDS WEIGH LESS THAN A PENNY

# *44

A hummingbird is the smallest of all birds. Some are no bigger than your thumb—and that includes the bill. These tiny birds are also great flyers. They can stay in one place in the air and fly forward, backward, sideways, or upside down. The birds got their name from the whirring sound their wings make as they dart through the air.

A hyena's laugh is really a cry, or howl, that the animal makes during a hunt. Hyenas usually search for prey in packs and use their whooping laughs to keep in touch. But laughing is not the only scary sound that hyenas make. A frightened hyena may also scream, groan, growl, or moan.

# #45
## HYENAS LAUGH WHEN THEY CRY

# #46 AN IGUANA'S TAIL IS LONGER THAN ITS BODY

The iguana's long tail is very useful. It helps the lizard keep its balance and swim fast in the water. If attacked, the iguana uses its tail like a whip. There are many kinds of iguanas. But all of them have scaly bodies, five toes on each foot, long sharp claws, and tails that are more than half of their overall length.

A jellyfish is a medusa (meh-DOO-suh), not a fish—even though it swims in the ocean. Its squishy body looks like it is made of jelly. Hanging down from its body are long strings that shoot out tiny poison darts. As soon as a dart touches a small fish or other sea animal, the strings pull up the victim—and the jellyfish gets something to eat.

A JELLYFISH IS NOT A FISH

47

# 48 A KANGAROO IS FASTER THAN A RACEHORSE

Kangaroos can reach speeds as high as 43 miles an hour (70 kph) with their long, strong back legs. But kangaroos don't run. They hop. To speed up, a kangaroo doesn't hop faster. It just takes longer hops. A kangaroo in a hurry can cross a river as wide as a tennis court in only one leap. It can reach a basketball hoop in a single jump.

Killer whales mostly kill and eat fish, squid, seals, and birds. Sometimes they even attack whales bigger than themselves. But killer whales do not prey on humans. These whales, which are also called orcas, usually hunt in packs. They are very fast swimmers and can have bursts of speed as high as 30 miles an hour (48.4 kph).

# #49 KILLER WHALES DON'T KILL PEOPLE

# #50 KOALAS ARE FUSSY EATERS

Koalas (koh-AH-luhz) eat only one food—the leaves of the gum, or eucalyptus, tree. A baby koala is like a baby kangaroo. It stays in a pouch on its mother's body for about six months. Once it leaves the pouch, its only food is gum-tree leaves. The leaves contain all the water a koala needs. No wonder the animal's name means "no water."

Lions are not the largest, strongest, or fastest of the big cats. Tigers are larger, leopards are stronger, and cheetahs are faster. Nor do all lions live in the jungle. Most make their homes on open, grassy plains. Their brownish yellow fur, which is the color of dry grass, helps them to hide while they hunt.

LIONS ARE NOT "KINGS OF THE JUNGLE"

#51

# #52 LIZARDS CAN LOSE THEIR TAILS—AND GROW NEW ONES

Many lizards are attacked by animals that bite off their tails. Snap! The lizard's tail falls to the ground. Yet the lizard needs a tail to keep its balance as it walks or climbs. Luckily for most lizards, a new tail grows back to take the place of the old one.

Mayflies have no mouths and do not take in food. That's because they have such short lives. Most mayflies live less than one day. In fact, one kind of mayfly has a life span of fewer than five minutes. Some mayflies just lay eggs—and then die.

# #53 A MAYFLY NEVER EATS

# #54 MOLES ARE NEARLY BLIND

Most moles spend their entire lives under the ground. Their very small eyes are of little use in the dark tunnels, or burrows, where moles live. But moles have a good sense of smell and touch. Hairs on their noses and tails help them get around in the dark and find worms and insects to eat.

Many monkeys have useful "thumbs" on their hands *and* their feet. These thumbs are much like your thumbs. They let monkeys grab and hold almost anything. They can peel bananas, catch insects, comb bugs out of their fur, and swing at high speeds from tree to tree.

# 55 A MONKEY'S BIG TOE WORKS LIKE YOUR THUMB

# 56 MOSQUITOES DON'T BITE

Mosquitoes have no jaws, no teeth, and no mouth. Therefore, they cannot bite. Instead, female mosquitoes stab their victims with a long tube that has six tiny, pointed needles inside. The mosquitoes sip the blood through the tube and fly away. The females need the blood to make their eggs.

Many people think that moths eat wool and leave little holes. But that's not what happens. A female adult moth lays her eggs on things made of wool. The eggs hatch into tiny caterpillars. And it is the hungry caterpillars that eat the wool and make tiny holes. Later, the caterpillars change into adult moths.

# #57 MOTHS DON'T MAKE MOTH HOLES

# #58 AN OCTOPUS HAS NO BONES

An octopus has eight arms—but no bones or shell. Its soft body is protected by a tough outside covering, called a mantle. The only hard parts of its body are its strong jaws, which come together to form a small beak. The octopus scoots along by taking water into its body and then forcing it out again.

When threatened, an opossum will sometimes play dead. The opossum makes its body soft and floppy. It opens its mouth, lets its tongue hang out, and hardly breathes at all. Many predator animals will not eat a dead opossum. So away they go. Then the "dead" opossum springs back to life.

# 59 OPOSSUMS CAN PLAY DEAD

# 60 ORANGUTANS USE TOOLS

Orangutans are apes that use simple tools, much as you do. A long stick is a favorite tool. The orangutan pokes the stick into an ant nest and licks off the insects that come out. If the stick has a point, the orangutan uses it to break through the thick skin of fruits it likes to eat. Of course, the stick also makes a great back scratcher.

An ostrich is taller than a grown man and weighs more than twice as much. A kick with one of the ostrich's long legs has the power of a boxer's punch. Also, the ostrich can cut a victim with its very long, sharp toenails. The old story that ostriches hide their heads in the sand is false. They never do.

# #61 AN OSTRICH HAS A KILLER KICK

# #62 OWLS CAN TURN THEIR HEADS AROUND

An owl's eyes face forward, not to the sides like most birds. But an owl cannot move its eyes. To see in other directions, the owl must turn its head. Luckily, an owl has 14 neck bones, not seven as you do. This makes it easy for the bird to twist its head all around.

A panda has five fingers on each front paw. But each paw also has a wrist bone that works like an extra thumb. This bone lets the panda hold bamboo as tightly as you can hold a toothbrush. Pandas spend up to 16 hours a day eating bamboo, which is just about their only food.

A PANDA HAS EXTRA "THUMBS" ON ITS FRONT PAWS

63

# 64 PANTHERS ARE BLACK LEOPARDS

Most leopards have tan fur with black spots. But the coats of some leopards are so dark that you can't see the spots. The spots are invisible. These leopards are called panthers. Jaguars with black fur are also known as panthers. Mountain lions, pumas, and cougars are different names for large, black cats. They, too, are sometimes called panthers. In short, a panther can be *any* big cat that has dark fur.

A mother penguin lays an egg on land and leaves to find food in the ocean. The father penguin then rolls the egg on top of his feet to keep it warm. For about two months, the father warms the egg. He has nothing to eat and grows very thin. When the egg hatches, the mother returns with food for the baby—and the father leaves to look for food.

# #65 EMPEROR PENGUIN FATHERS HATCH THE EGGS

# #66 PIGEONS DO NOT DRINK WATER LIKE OTHER BIRDS

Most birds sip water, but don't swallow it. They just tilt their heads back and let the water flow down their throats. Only pigeons drink water and pump it down their throats, just as you do. Pigeons are at home in the city or the country. They find water to sip—and swallow—no matter where they live.

Plover birds hop inside the crocodiles' mouths. But the crocodiles do not harm them. That's because the birds peck bits of food stuck in the crocodiles' teeth. Some plovers also pick off the pesky insects that land on the crocodiles' backs. As the plovers help the crocodiles, they also feed themselves.

PLOVERS CLEAN CROCODILES' TEETH

67

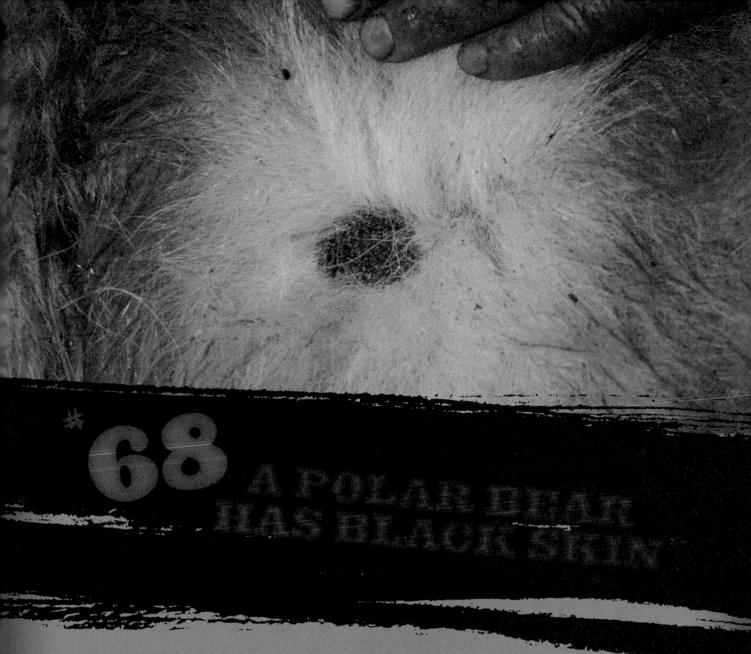

# #68 A POLAR BEAR HAS BLACK SKIN

The polar bear looks white or cream-colored. But its skin is black. The bear's black skin absorbs the sun's rays while its long, white hairs trap the body's heat. Together, the dark skin and the thick coat of fur help keep the animal warm, no matter how cold it gets.

A pony is a kind of horse that grows older—but never grows very big. The Shetland is a well-known type of pony. When it is fully grown, a Shetland is nearly 2 feet (0.6 m) shorter than most other kinds of horses. We call a young male horse a colt and a female a filly.

# #69 A PONY IS NOT A YOUNG HORSE

# #70 PORCUPINES DON'T SHOOT THEIR QUILLS

A porcupine has thousands of long, pointed quills on its body and tail. Most of the time, the quills lie flat, hidden by long, dark hairs. But sometimes a lion, dog, or other enemy attacks. The porcupine pops up its quills, backs up, and swings its tail. Even though it doesn't shoot the quills, some jab into the enemy. Ouch!

When two prairie dogs meet, it looks as if they are kissing. Actually, they are just touching teeth. They do this to find out if they are from the same family group. If they are, the two prairie dogs clean each other's fur. If not, they fight, and one drives the other away.

# #71 PRAIRIE DOGS "KISS" WHEN THEY MEET

# #72 A PYTHON CAN SWALLOW A DEER

Pythons can open their mouths wide enough to swallow prey much bigger than themselves. Often, a python catches a large animal and sinks its teeth into the victim's body. Then the snake coils its body around the prey and squeezes hard until the animal stops breathing. Finally, the python swallows the dead prey whole.

Raccoons often swish their hands around in shallow water. It may look like they are washing their food. But don't believe it. Most likely, they're looking for a frog, turtle, or fish to eat. Or they may be dipping dry food in the water to make it easy to swallow.

# #73 RACCOONS DON'T WASH THEIR FOOD

# RATTLESNAKES RATTLE BEFORE THEY BITE

## #74

When in danger, a rattlesnake shakes its tail back and forth. The loose, hornlike rings at the end of its tail hit against each other. This makes a rattling sound that can frighten almost any animal—or person. "Go away," it warns. If not, the rattlesnake is ready to attack and bite with its poisonous fangs.

All reindeer lose their antlers every year and grow new ones. Females drop their antlers in the spring and grow new ones right away. Males, on the other hand, shed their antlers in November or December. Then new ones start to grow.

#75

REINDEER LOSE THEIR ANTLERS EVERY YEAR

# #76 RHINOCEROSES USE SUNSCREEN

On hot days, rhinoceroses bathe in muddy water. When the mud dries on them, it forms a kind of sunscreen. Mud shields the rhino's skin from the sun's harmful rays. It also cools the rhino and wards off bites from annoying insects. Do you think rhino moms cover their young with mud before they go out to play?

To "see red" means to get very angry. When a male robin sees the red breast of another male, it "sees red." A male robin often attacks any outsider that comes into its territory. Sometimes it charges its own reflection in a big window. Or it may even peck at a red rag hanging in a tree.

# #77 ROBINS SOMETIMES "SEE RED"

# #78 ROOSTERS CROW MORNING, NOON, AND NIGHT

You may think that roosters only crow in the morning. That's not so. Roosters crow any time of the day. They crow to signal danger, to express surprise, or just for the fun of it. You may notice the rooster's crow at dawn because there are few other sounds at that hour. It's often the first thing you hear in the morning.

Female salmon swim up freshwater rivers to lay their eggs. In a few months the eggs hatch. The young salmon then swim downriver to the saltwater ocean. They live there for a year or more. Then they swim back up the river where they were born. The next generation of females now lays its eggs—and everything starts all over again.

**79** SALMON ARE BORN IN FRESH WATER, BUT LIVE IN SALT WATER

# #80 SEA HORSE DADS HATCH THE EGGS

A female sea horse lays her eggs inside a male sea horse's pouch. She swims away and the eggs hatch in his pouch. The baby sea horses swim out. Most of them wrap their tails around seaweed and stay in one place. They grab—and eat—any small sea creatures that swim by. A sea horse is named for its head, which looks like a tiny horse's head.

Seaweed grows up from the ocean bottom. Sea otters wrap themselves in the seaweed to keep from being carried away by ocean waves. The seaweed keeps them in one place as they float on their backs and go to sleep. It also keeps them from drifting away as they dine on clams, crabs, or starfish—their favorite foods.

# SEA OTTERS WRAP THEMSELVES IN SEAWEED

# #81

# #82 SOME SEALS DON'T HAVE EXTERNAL EARS

Many seals can hear very well—even though they don't have external ears. Their good sense of hearing comes from two tiny ear openings behind the eyes. The little holes may be hard for you to see. But sounds pass in through these small openings and let the seal hear even the softest sounds.

Shark teeth are not in a single row like your teeth. They form a few rows, one behind the other. When a shark bites, its front teeth often fall out or break off. But a day or two later, new teeth from behind move up to take their places. A single shark can lose—and grow—as many as 20,000 teeth in its lifetime.

83 SHARKS HAVE THOUSANDS OF TEETH

# #84 SHEEP WALK RIGHT AFTER THEY ARE BORN

In spring, female sheep (ewes) give birth to one or two babies (lambs). Within a few minutes, the lambs get up on their four legs and start to walk. The lambs drink milk from the ewe's body. Before long, they are part of the flock, running and leaping with the others.

When an enemy comes close, the skunk stamps its front feet and hisses loudly. Sometimes that's enough to scare the enemy away. Otherwise, the skunk may raise its tail, turn around, and spray an awful-smelling liquid into the air. The terrible odor can be picked up as far away as a mile (1.6 km). And it lasts for many days.

# #85 A SKUNK'S SMELL TRAVELS FAR

# #86 SLOTHS LIVE UPSIDE DOWN

Sloths eat, sleep, mate, have babies, and die the same way—hanging upside down in a tree. They hold on to the branches with their claws and creep along so slowly that it seems they are not moving at all. In fact, sloths sleep for about 17 hours every day. They spend the rest of the time looking—very slowly—for leaves to eat.

Almost every snake is born with a single body and head. But now and then a snake with one body and *two* heads comes along. A rat snake with two heads named "We" lived at the World Aquarium in St. Louis for 8 years. Millions of visitors saw it before it died there in June 2007.

# #87 SOME SNAKES HAVE TWO HEADS

# #88 SPIDERS ARE NOT INSECTS

Spiders are not insects like flies, ants, bees, and butterflies. They are arachnids (uh-RAK-nids), along with ticks, mites, scorpions, and daddy longlegs. Spiders have eight legs; insects have six. Spiders have two body parts; insects have three. And finally, spiders don't have wings or feelers; most insects do.

Squirrels gather lots of nuts, acorns, bulbs, and seeds at the end of summer. The animals dig small holes and bury the food for winter. But, come the cold weather, most squirrels can't find the food that they buried. Instead, they dig up food that other squirrels hid underground—and that tastes just as good.

# SQUIRRELS RARELY FIND THE NUTS THEY BURY IN THE FALL

# #89

# #90 STARFISH PUSH THEIR STOMACHS THROUGH THEIR MOUTHS

Starfish eat shellfish—clams, oysters, and mussels—in an odd way. The starfish attaches the suckers on its five legs to the animal's shells. Slowly it forces the shells apart. When the opening is big enough, the starfish shoves in its stomach. The stomach digests the flesh of the shellfish. Then the starfish swallows its full stomach.

There are no wild tigers in Africa, or any other continent except Asia. A century ago, Asia was home to about 100,000 tigers. Today, though, there are only about 4,000 remaining in the wild. Human hunting and loss of habitat are to blame for the huge drop in tiger numbers. But about 9,000 of these big cats now live in zoos, in circuses, and on tiger "farms."

# 91 WILD TIGERS LIVE ONLY IN ASIA

## 92 A BABY TURTLE NEVER SEES ITS MOTHER

A female turtle lays as many as 200 eggs in a hole she digs in the ground. She covers the eggs with soil or sand—and goes away. Two or three months later, the eggs hatch. The baby turtles break free and rush off to a safe place. They must hurry before they're caught by a predator.

Vampire bats lap up blood with their tongues. But they don't *suck* blood. The bats have razor-sharp teeth. They usually use the teeth to make tiny cuts in the skins of sleeping horses or cattle. The bats then quickly lap up the drops of blood that form. Before the victim wakes, the vampire bats dart away into the night sky.

# #93

# VAMPIRE BATS DON'T SUCK BLOOD

# #94 VULTURES ONLY EAT DEAD ANIMALS

Vultures fly very high in the sky. They float on air currents, looking for the remains of dead animals on the ground. When they spot one, they swoop down to pick at the meat. Vultures will eat any animal killed by disease, other animals, hunters, or cars.

A baby walrus starts to grow tusks when it's about one year old. Each tusk can become a yard (1 m) long. The walrus uses its tusks to do everything from making holes in the ice to digging for clams in the ocean bottom. Tusks also help the walrus climb out of the water. The walrus with the longest tusks often becomes the leader of its group.

# 95 A WALRUS'S TUSKS ARE ITS TWO FRONT TEETH

# #96 WASPS THAT LIVE TOGETHER BUILD PAPER NESTS

Wasps that live together are called social wasps. They build their nests in trees or the corners of houses, barns, or other buildings. To start, the social wasps chew tiny bits of wood into pulp. They shape the pulp into nests with many small rooms, or cells. As the pulp dries, it turns into paper. Wasps build new nests every year.

Whales are mammals. So are dogs and cats, lions and tigers, and humans. Like almost all mammals, a whale grows inside its mother's body. A baby whale is called a calf. The mother pushes the calf to the surface to get its first breath of air. Up until one year of age, the calf drinks milk from its mother's body.

# #97 A WHALE IS NOT A FISH

# #98 A WHALE SHARK IS THE BIGGEST FISH

A whale shark is about the size of a large school bus. Yet it feeds on the tiniest plants and animals in the sea. This giant fish bobs up and down in the water with its mouth wide open. Huge amounts of water—and food—flow in. The whale shark then forces the water out through openings in the sides of its head. What's left is dinner.

Smell is the wolf's strongest sense. Its long snout can pick up smells that you would not even notice. A wolf sniffs the air to find large prey, such as moose or deer. But wolves also have excellent hearing. To find smaller prey, such as rabbits, mice, and squirrels, wolves mainly listen for their sounds.

# 99 A WOLF CAN PICK UP SMELLS 100 TIMES BETTER THAN YOU

# #100 WORMS HAVE NO EYES, EARS, OR NOSE

Common worms, or earthworms, cannot see, hear, or smell. But they do have a good sense of touch. The worms can tell the difference between hard and soft, hot and cold, dry and wet. They can also tell light from dark. Even without eyes, ears, or a nose, earthworms can tunnel through the ground and find the rotting leaves on which they feed.

A busy pattern of black or dark brown stripes helps zebras hide—even on the open plains where most live. Zebras usually move in groups. The stripes make it hard to pick out one zebra from all the rest. This confuses lions and other enemies—and helps the zebras survive. No two zebras have exactly the same pattern of stripes.

# #101 ZEBRAS HIDE IN PLAIN SIGHT

# INDEX

# PHOTO CREDITS

Front cover: (elephant, koala, lemur, nutria, hamster, zebra, koi, cat, frog, macaque, tiger, gorilla) Eric Isselee/Shutterstock (pig) Jokter/Shutterstock (polar bear) Keith Levit/Shutterstock; Page 4t: Bruce Coleman/BCIUSA; Page 4b: Pixtal/age fotostock; Page 5t: Fritz Polking/Peter Arnold, Inc.; Page 5b: Todd S. Holder/Shutterstock; Page 6t: Shutterstock; Page 6b: J. M. Horrillo/age fotostock; Page 7t: Bruce Coleman/BCIUSA; Page 7b: Michael Ledray/Shutterstock; Page 8t: Rick & Nora Bowers/Alamy; Page 8b: Jim Zuckerman/Alamy; Page 9t: Joe McDonald/Animals Animals; Page 9b: Joe McDonald/Animals Animals; Page 10t: Javarman/Shutterstock; Page 10b: Michael Durham/Minden Pictures; Page 11t: Alamy; Page 11b: Rob Byron/Shutterstock; Page 12t: Tischenko Irina/Shutterstock; Page 12b: John B. Free/Minden Pictures; Page 13t: Bruce Coleman/BCIUSA; Page 13b: SeaPics; Page 14t: Olivier Le Queinec/Shutterstock; Page 14b: Juniors Bildarchiv/Alamy; Page 15t: SUNNYphotography.com/Alamy; Page 15b: Inaki Antonana Plaza/Shutterstock; Page 16t:

Neale Cousland/Shutterstock; Page 16b: Papilio/Alamy; Page 17t: Juniors Bildarchiv/Alamy; Page 17b: Javarman/Shutterstock; Page 18t: Brian Morrison/Shutterstock; Page 18b: Visual&Written SL/Alamy; Page 19t: Papilio/Alamy; Page 19b: Johnny Tran/Shutterstock; Page 20t: Sebastian Duda/Shutterstock; Page 20b: Art Wolfe/Photo Researchers, Inc.; Page 21t: Gerard Lacz/Animals Animals; Page 21b: Eric Gevaert/Shutterstock; Page 22t: Emily Goodwin/Shutterstock; Page 22b: Agripicture Images/Alamy; Page 23t & back cover: Steve Bloom Images/Alamy; Page 23b: Jong Kiam Soon/Shutterstock; Page 24t: EcoPrint/Shutterstock; Page 24b: Frédéric Soltan/Sygma/Corbis; Page 25t: Anthony Bannister/Animals Animals; Page 25b: Liewwk/Shutterstock; Page 26t: Eric Isselee/Shutterstock; Page 26b: Maximilian Weinzierl/Alamy; Page 27t: WoodyStock/Alamy; Page 27b: Arco Images GmbH/Alamy; Page 28t: Aleksandar-Pal Sakala/Shutterstock; Page 28b: Roger Harris/Photo Researchers, Inc.; Page 29t: Arco Images GmbH/Alamy; Page 29b: Naomi Hasegawa/

Shutterstock; Page 30t: Jenny Solomon/Shutterstock; Page 30b: Darby Sawchuk/Alamy; Page 31t: Arco Images GmbH/Alamy; Page 31b: Alle/Shutterstock; Page 32t: R. Gino Santa Maria/Shutterstock; Page 32b: Fritz Polking/Peter Arnold, Inc.; Page 33t: Darby Sawchuk/Alamy; Page 33b: Shutterstock; Page 34t: Anita Patterson Peppers/Shutterstock; Page 34b: Phil Degginger/Alamy; Page 35t: Fabio Colombini Medeiros/Animals Animals; Page 35b: StudioNewmarket/Shutterstock; Page 36t: blickwinkel/Alamy; Page 36b: SeaPics; Page 37t: Zigmund Leszczynski/Animals Animals; Page 37b: Martin Valigursky/Shutterstock; Page 38t: Brad Thompson/Shutterstock; Page 38b: Sz Akos/Shutterstock; Page 39t: age fotostock; Page 39b: Ivonne Wierink/Shutterstock; Page 40t: Eric Isselee/Shutterstock; Page 40b: Superstock/age fotostock; Page 41t: Arco Images GmbH/Alamy; Page 41b: Heather A. Craig/Shutterstock; Page 42t: Eric Isselee/Shutterstock; Page 42b: BIOS/Peter Arnold, Inc.; Page 43t & back cover: Biosphoto/Puillandre Roger/Peter Arnold, Inc.; Page 43b: Eric Isselee/Shutterstock; Page 44t: Allyson Ricketts/Shutterstock; Page 44b: Raymond Mendez/Animals Animals; Page 45t: Esa Hiltula/Alamy; Page 45b: Karen Givens/Shutterstock; Page 46t: Stephen Meese/Shutterstock; Page 46b: Juniors Bildarchiv/Alamy; Page 47t: Bob Gaspari/Alamy; Page 47b: idesign/Shutterstock; Page 48t: Eric Isselee/Shutterstock; Page 48b: F1online digitale Bildagentur GmbH/Alamy; Page 49t: TUNS/Peter Arnold, Inc.; Page 49b: Lori Martin/Shutterstock; Page 50t: Mark William Penny/Shutterstock; Page 50b: SeaPics; Page 51t: Dave Watts/Alamy; Page 51b: Henk Bentlage/Shutterstock; Page 52t: George Burba/Shutterstock; Page 52b: SeaPics; Page 53t: PCL/Alamy; Page 53b: John Austin/Shutterstock; Page 54t: JKlingebiel/Shutterstock; Page 54b: Hamman/Heldring/Animals Animals; Page 55t: Zigmund Leszczynski/Animals Animals; Page 55b: Eric Isselee/Shutterstock; Page 56t: Steve Mann/Shutterstock; Page 56b: blickwinkel/Alamy; Page 57t: Leonard Lee Rue III/BCIUSA; Page 57b: Tramper/Shutterstock; Page 58t: Eric Isselee/Shutterstock; Page 58b: Panoramic Images/Getty Images; Page 59t & back cover: Richard T. Nowitz/Corbis; Page 59b: Yaroslav/Shutterstock; Page 60t: Cathy Keifer/Shutterstock; Page 60b: Nigel Cattlin/Alamy; Page 61t: SeaPics; Page 61b: John A. Anderson/Shutterstock; Page 62t: Teekaygee/Shutterstock; Page 62b: Michael Habicht/Animals Animals; Page 63t: Jonathan Hewitt/Alamy; Page 63b: Olga Sweet/Shutterstock; Page 64t: Trutta55/Shutterstock; Page 64b: Bernd Settnik/dpa/Corbis; Page 65t: Stock Image/Jupiterimage; Page 65b: Laurent Renault/Shutterstock; Page 66t: Biosphoto/Ruoso Cyril/Peter Arnold, Inc.; Page 66b: StockPile Collection/Alamy; Page 67t: age fotostock; Page 67b: Eric Gevaert/Shutterstock; Page 68t: Jan Martin Will/Shutterstock; Page 68b: Biosphoto/Blanc Samuel/

Peter Arnold, Inc.; Page 69t: O.S.F./ Animals Animals; Page 69b: Mykhalio Zhelezniak/Shutterstock; Page 70t: Dennis Donohue/Shutterstock; Page 70b & back cover: Juniors Bildarchiv/ age fotostock; Page 71t: Sue Flood/ Nature Picture Library; Page 71b: Keith Levit/Shutterstock; Page 72t: Cynoclub/Shutterstock; Page 72b: Cheryl Engel/Alamy; Page 73t: Alaska Stock LLC/Alamy; Page 73b: Poprugin Aleksey/Shutterstock; Page 74t: Eric Gevaert/Shutterstock; Page 74b: Gordon & Cathy Illg/ Animals Animals; Page 75t: Gunter Ziesler/Peter Arnold, Inc.; Page 75b: Anita Patterson Peppers/ Shutterstock; Page 76t: Eric Isselee/ Shutterstock; Page 76b: tbkmedia. de/Alamy; Page 77t: Rick & Nora Bowers/Alamy; Page 77b: Casey K. Bishop/Shutterstock; Page 78t: Andreas Gradin/Shutterstock; Page 78b: Arco Images GmbH/Alamy; Page 79t: Terry Whittaker/Alamy; Page 79b: Karen Givens/Shutterstock; Page 80t: Michael J. Thompson/ Shutterstock; Page 80b: Keith M. Law/Alamy; Page 81t: age fotostock; Page 81b: Marina Cano Trueba/ Shutterstock; Page 82t: Tischenko Irina/Shutterstock; Page 82b: Steve Bloom Images/Alamy; Page 83t: SeaPics; Page 83b: Radovan Spurny/Shutterstock; Page 84t: Heather Dillion/Shutterstock; Page 84b & back cover: Tom Mangelesen/ Nature Picture Library; Page 85t: age fotostock; Page 85b: Vladimir Meinik/Shutterstock; Page 86t: Ian Scott/Shutterstock; Page 86b & back cover: David Fleetham/Alamy; Page 87t: imagebroker/Alamy; Page 87b:

Lee Torrens/Shutterstock; Page 88t: Holly Kuchera/Shutterstock; Page 88b: Corbis Premium RF/Alamy; Page 89t: Stockbyte/Alamy; Page 89b: Timothy Craig Lubcke/Shutterstock; Page 90t: John R. MacGregor/Peter Arnold, Inc.; Page 90b: Bill Beatty/ Animals Animals; Page 91t & back cover: Peter Arnold, Inc.; Page 91b: Aliciahh/Shutterstock; Page 92t: Bruce MacQueen/Shutterstock; Page 92b: David Norton/Alamy; Page 93t: Peter Arnold, Inc.; Page 93b: Alvaro Pantoja/Shutterstock; Page 94t: Eric Isselee/Shutterstock; Page 94b: Biosphoto/Allofs Theo/Peter Arnold, Inc.; Page 95t: Aqua Image/Alamy; Page 95b: Visual&Written SL/Alamy; Page 96t: Javarman/Shutterstock; Page 96b: Michael Fogden/Animals Animals; Page 97t: Jose B. Ruiz/ Nature Picture Library; Page 97b: Lars Christensen/Shutterstock; Page 98t: Gail Johnson/ Shutterstock; Page 98b: SeaPics; Page 99t: Dennis MacDonald/ Alamy; Page 99b: StudioNewmarket/ Shutterstock; Page 100t: Brett Atkins/Shutterstock; Page 100b: SeaPics; Page 101t: SeaPics; Page 101b: SeaPics; Page 102t: Geoffrey Kuchera/Shutterstock; Page 102b: Ingram Publishing (Superstock Limited)/Alamy; Page 103t: Peter Arnold,, Inc./Alamy; Page 103b: Creative Images/Shutterstock; Page 104t: Chris Fouris/Shutterstock; Page 104b: Biosphoto/Pons Alain/ Peter Arnold, Inc.; Back cover: (giraffe) Mark Higgins/Alamy.